Real Estate Law Essentials
Navigate Transactions, Avoid Pitfalls, and Seize Opportunities

By Willem Tait

Copyright © 2024 by Willem Tait
All rights reserved.

No part of this publication may be reproduced, distributed, or transmitted in any form or by any means, including photocopying, recording, or other electronic or mechanical methods, without the prior written permission of the author, except in the case of brief quotations embodied in reviews and certain other noncommercial uses permitted by copyright law.

For permission requests, contact the author at:
willemtait@gmail.com

This book is for educational and informational purposes only. The author is not liable for any damages or losses arising from the use or misuse of the content in this book.

Cover Design: Time Brands
Published by WRT Publishing

First Edition

KDP AMAZON ISBN: 9798302431189
ISBN Ebook: 978-0-6398577-5-6
ISBN Print: 978-0-6398577-4-9

Introduction: Unlocking the Doors to Real Estate Law

Imagine navigating a world where every property decision you make, whether buying your dream home, investing in real estate, or managing rental properties, feels confident, informed, and secure. In the complex world of real estate, the law is the foundation upon which every transaction, negotiation, and ownership decision is built. Yet for many, understanding the intricacies of real estate law feels like an overwhelming maze, full of unfamiliar terms and high-stakes decisions.

That's where this book comes in. *Real Estate Law Essentials* is your comprehensive guide to the legal principles that shape the U.S. property market. Whether you're a seasoned investor, a first-time homebuyer, or a professional seeking to deepen your knowledge, this book is designed to make complex legal concepts accessible and actionable. It's more than just a **book**, it's a key that unlocks the doors to understanding how to protect your rights, maximize your investments, and avoid costly mistakes.

What makes this book different? It's not a dry legal manual filled with jargon and fine print. Instead, it's a practical, reader-friendly guide packed with real-world scenarios, clear explanations, and insights that bridge the gap between theory and practice. Each chapter is crafted to not only educate but also engage, taking you step-by-step through the essential elements of property law.

By the time you've turned the last page, you'll have the confidence to make informed decisions in any real estate transaction. You'll understand the rights and responsibilities of ownership, the intricacies of contracts, the nuances of zoning, and so much more. With this book in hand, you won't just learn about real estate law, you'll master it.

So, whether you're standing at the threshold of your first property deal or looking to refine your expertise, this is where your journey begins. Turn the page, and let's open the door to a world of knowledge that will empower you to succeed in real estate.

Why Understanding Real Estate Law Really Matters

When it comes to real estate, every decision you make has consequences, financial, legal, and even emotional. Whether you're negotiating a big deal, buying your first home, managing a rental property portfolio, or investing in commercial real estate, the law plays a critical role in protecting your interests and shaping the outcome of your actions. But here's the secret: understanding real estate law doesn't have to be overwhelming.

This book is designed to take you from confusion to clarity. By learning the foundational principles of property law, you'll gain the tools to confidently navigate transactions, avoid common pitfalls, and seize opportunities with ease. You'll understand not just *what* to do, but *why* it matters, empowering you to make smarter, more informed decisions at every turn.

Think of this as your personal guidebook, a comprehensive resource designed to demystify the complexities of real estate law and present them in simple, actionable steps. Real estate, with all its legal, financial, and logistical layers, can feel overwhelming at first. But with the right guidance, those complexities transform into opportunities. This book isn't just about learning the rules, it's about empowering you to make informed decisions and confidently navigate every aspect of your real estate journey.

Whether you're a landlord managing rental properties, a tenant looking to protect your rights, a buyer making one of the biggest financial decisions of your life, or a seller aiming to maximise returns, this guide equips you with practical knowledge and strategies tailored to your needs. From understanding contracts and zoning regulations to mastering dispute resolution and avoiding common pitfalls, every chapter is crafted to give you an edge in the competitive world of real estate.

The more you understand, the greater your advantage. Knowledge isn't just power, it's the foundation for success. With every concept you grasp and every strategy you implement, you'll be one step closer to achieving your real estate goals. Ready to gain that edge, take control of your future, and turn challenges into opportunities? Let's dive in and begin your journey toward real estate mastery.

Table of Contents

Introduction: Unlocking the Doors to Real Estate Law 2
Why Understanding Real Estate Law Really Matters 4
Table of Contents 6
Chapter 1: Introduction to Real Estate Law 14
    The Importance of Real Estate Law 14
    The Scope of Real Estate Law 15
    Key Concepts in Real Estate Law 17
    The Legal Foundations of Real Estate Law............19
    Conclusion: Building a Foundation for Success 21
Chapter 2: Understanding Property Ownership 22
    Introduction to Property Ownership 22
    Types of Property Ownership 23
        Freehold Ownership 23
        Leasehold Ownership 24
    Ownership Responsibilities....................................26
        Maintenance and Upkeep 26
        Financial Obligations 27
        Community and Environmental Impact.............27
    Limitations on Ownership: Zoning Laws and Easements..28
        Zoning Laws 28
        Easements...29
    Conclusion: Navigating Property Ownership 30
Chapter 3: Navigating Real Estate Transactions.....32
    Introduction to Real Estate Transactions................32

Step One: Preparing for a Real Estate Transaction 33
    Understanding Your Goals 33
    Researching the Market....................................34
    Securing Financing 34
Step Two: Conducting a Title Search 35
    What is a Title Search?.....................................35
    Common Title Issues 36
Step Three: Drafting and Negotiating the Contract.37
    Key Components of a Real Estate Contract 37
    Negotiating the Terms 38
Step Four: Closing the Transaction 38
    The Closing Process...39
    Common Closing Challenges 39
Step Five: Post-Transaction Considerations 40
    For Buyers 40
    For Sellers 40
Conclusion: Mastering Real Estate Transactions ...41

Chapter 4: Real Estate Contracts and Agreements 44
Introduction to Real Estate Contracts 44
Key Components of Real Estate Contracts 45
    Offer and Acceptance 45
    Consideration..46
    Legal Purpose and Competence 46
Understanding Contingency Clauses 47
    Common Contingencies 47
    Balancing Contingencies 48
Negotiation Strategies 49
    Preparing for Negotiation..................................49

    Effective Communication 50
    Leveraging Contract Terms 50
Ensuring Legal Enforceability 51
    Clarity and Specificity 51
    Written Agreements 51
    Signatures and Witnesses 52
    Compliance with Local Laws 52
Conclusion: Mastering Real Estate Agreements 53

Chapter 5: Zoning and Land Use Regulations 56
Introduction to Zoning and Land Use 56
The Legal Framework of Zoning Laws 57
    The Purpose of Zoning 57
    Legal Authority 58
Zoning Classifications 59
    Residential Zoning 59
    Commercial Zoning 60
    Industrial Zoning 60
    Special Zoning Categories 61
Land Use Restrictions 61
    Easements 61
    Covenants 62
    Environmental Regulations 62
Resolving Zoning Disputes 63
    Common Causes of Zoning Disputes 63
    Strategies for Resolution 64
Conclusion: Mastering Zoning and Land Use 65

Chapter 6: Mortgages, Financing, and Liens 67
Introduction to Real Estate Financing 67
Understanding Mortgages 68

Components of a Mortgage 68
Types of Mortgages 69
The Role of Liens in Real Estate 70
Types of Liens 70
Implications of Liens 71
Navigating Foreclosure 72
The Foreclosure Process 72
Avoiding Foreclosure 73
Borrowers' Rights and Obligations 74
Borrowers' Rights 74
Borrowers' Obligations 75
Practical Advice for Navigating Financing 76
Assess Your Financial Situation 76
Shop Around for Lenders 76
Understand the Fine Print 76
Plan for the Long Term 77
Conclusion: Mastering Real Estate Financing 77
Chapter 7: Legal Issues in Rental Properties 80
Introduction to Legal Issues in Rental Properties ... 80
The Foundation of Landlord-Tenant Relationships . 81
Key Rights of Tenants 81
Key Rights of Landlords 82
Lease Agreements: The Cornerstone of Rental
Relationships 83
Key Components of a Lease Agreement 83
Legal Requirements for Leases 85
Common Disputes in Rental Properties 85
Nonpayment of Rent 86
Maintenance and Repairs 86

Security Deposit Disputes 87
Resolving Rental Disputes 87
    Communication and Negotiation 87
    Mediation 88
    Legal Action 88
Rights and Responsibilities of Each Party 89
    Landlord Responsibilities 89
    Tenant Responsibilities 90
Conclusion: Navigating Legal Issues in Rental Properties 90

Chapter 8: Dispute Resolution and Future Trends .94
Introduction to Dispute Resolution and Future Trends 94
Methods of Resolving Real Estate Disputes 95
    Mediation: Collaborative Problem-Solving 95
    The Mediation Process 97
        Benefits of Mediation 97
    Arbitration: A Middle Ground 98
        The Arbitration Process 98
        Benefits and Drawbacks 99
Litigation: The Courtroom Approach 100
    The Litigation Process 100
    Pros and Cons of Litigation 101
Emerging Trends in Real Estate Law 101
    Technological Innovations 101
    Blockchain Technology 102
    Artificial Intelligence (AI) 102
    Virtual Reality (VR) 103
Sustainability-Focused Regulations 103

Green Building Standards..................................103
Renewable Energy Incentives 104
Climate Resilience Regulations......................104
Integrating Dispute Resolution and Future Trends
....105
Conclusion: Preparing for the Future of Real Estate
....106

Chapter 9: Common Mistakes to Avoid..................109
Introduction to Common Mistakes in Real Estate.109
Mistakes Landlords Often Make 110
   Inadequate Screening of Tenants....................110
      How to Avoid This Mistake........................110
   Poorly Written Lease Agreements 111
      How to Avoid This Mistake........................111
Mistakes Tenants Often Make 111
   Ignoring the Lease Terms 112
      How to Avoid This Mistake........................112
   Skipping the Move-In Inspection.....................112
      How to Avoid This Mistake........................113
Mistakes Buyers Often Make.................................113
   Skipping the Home Inspection 114
      How to Avoid This Mistake........................114
   Overextending Financially 114
      How to Avoid This Mistake........................115
Mistakes Sellers Often Make 115
   Overpricing the Property...................................115
      How to Avoid This Mistake........................116
   Neglecting to Stage the Property.....................116
      How to Avoid This Mistake........................116

General Legal Mistakes to Avoid 117
　Failing to Conduct a Title Search 117
　　How to Avoid This Mistake 117
　Ignoring Local Zoning Laws 118
　　How to Avoid This Mistake 118
Conclusion: Learning from Common Mistakes 119

Chapter 10: Final Thoughts and Summary of Main Points 122

Reflecting on the Journey Through Real Estate Law 122

Understanding the Importance of Real Estate Law 123

Mastering Property Ownership 124
Navigating Real Estate Transactions 125
Crafting Effective Contracts 126
Navigating Zoning and Land Use Regulations 127
Managing Mortgages, Financing, and Liens 128
Navigating Legal Issues in Rental Properties 129
Resolving Disputes and Embracing Future Trends 130
Learning from Common Mistakes 131
Final Takeaways 131

Acknowledgements 133
Glossary of Keywords 135
Author Bio 144
Social Profiles and Contact Info 145
Public Speaking, Mentorship, Consulting, Coaching 146
Upcoming Projects 148

We Value Your Feedback!......................................149
Portfolio of Books by Willem Tait...........................150

Chapter 1: Introduction to Real Estate Law

The Importance of Real Estate Law

Real estate law influences nearly every aspect of property ownership and transactions, yet many people overlook its significance until challenges arise. Whether you're buying a home, leasing an apartment, or investing in real estate, the legal framework protects your rights and ensures fair dealings. Without a proper understanding of these laws, even routine transactions can lead to costly mistakes or disputes.

Imagine a first-time homebuyer signing a purchase agreement without realizing it includes a clause waiving their right to a home inspection. Later, they discover severe structural issues that cost tens of thousands to repair, issues that could have been avoided with better legal knowledge. The importance of real estate law lies not only in safeguarding investments but also in empowering individuals to approach transactions with confidence.

For investors, real estate law offers a strategic advantage. Knowledge of tax laws can reduce liabilities, while an understanding of zoning regulations can reveal opportunities others might miss. For tenants, landlord-tenant law ensures protection from unfair practices, such as illegal evictions or unjust rent increases. The practical applications of real estate law are vast and extend far beyond property ownership.

The law doesn't just protect, it empowers. By understanding your rights and obligations, you can negotiate stronger deals, recognize red flags, and avoid costly disputes. Whether you're a buyer, seller, landlord, or tenant, real estate law provides the tools to navigate an increasingly complex market.

The Scope of Real Estate Law

The scope of real estate law is vast, touching on almost every aspect of property use, ownership, and transfer. At its core, it governs how land and buildings are bought, sold, developed, and maintained. While this legal framework may seem intimidating at first, breaking it into key categories makes it easier to understand and apply.

One of the most visible areas of real estate law is property ownership. Ownership rights determine what you can and cannot do with your property, whether it's building a home, leasing it out, or selling it to another party. But ownership is rarely absolute, zoning laws, easements, and environmental regulations often place limitations on how property can be used. For instance, a landowner planning to build a restaurant might find that local zoning laws restrict the area to residential use, forcing them to alter their plans.

Contracts form another essential area of real estate law. These agreements, whether for sales, leases, or mortgages, define the terms and conditions under which property changes hands. Without a legally binding contract, disputes are almost inevitable. Real estate contracts are highly specific, often including terms related to contingencies, closing costs, and inspection results.

Financing and mortgages also fall within the scope of real estate law. From understanding loan agreements to navigating foreclosure, the legalities surrounding real estate financing are critical for both borrowers and lenders. For example, a borrower unaware of prepayment penalties in their mortgage agreement could face unexpected costs when trying to pay off their loan early.

Dispute resolution is another crucial element. Conflicts over boundaries, contract terms, or zoning violations often require mediation, arbitration, or litigation to resolve. Understanding the scope of real estate law enables property owners, investors, and professionals to anticipate potential challenges and address them proactively.

Key Concepts in Real Estate Law

At the heart of real estate law are key concepts that serve as its building blocks: ownership rights, contracts, liens, and disclosure requirements. Each of these elements plays a fundamental role in shaping property transactions and ensuring fairness.

Ownership rights are the foundation of real estate law. They determine not only who owns a property but also what they can do with it. For example, a freehold estate grants full ownership, allowing the owner to use, sell, or lease the property as they wish. In contrast, a leasehold estate provides rights for a limited period, with restrictions often set by the property owner. Understanding the nuances of ownership rights is essential for anyone involved in property dealings.

Contracts are equally important. A legally binding contract protects all parties in a transaction, outlining terms such as the purchase price, contingencies, and timelines. For instance, a seller might include a contingency clause requiring the buyer to secure financing within 30 days. If the buyer fails to meet this condition, the seller has the right to cancel the contract. Without clear and enforceable contracts, disputes are almost inevitable.

Liens add another layer of complexity. These legal claims against a property secure payment for a debt, such as a mortgage or tax bill. A lien must be resolved before a property can be sold, often requiring negotiation between the lienholder and the property owner. For example, a homeowner with unpaid property taxes may face a tax lien, which could lead to foreclosure if not addressed promptly.

Disclosure requirements are another critical concept. Sellers are legally obligated to disclose known issues with a property, such as structural damage or environmental hazards. Failure to do so can lead to legal action, as buyers have a right to know what they're purchasing.

By mastering these key concepts, property owners and investors can navigate transactions with greater confidence and protect themselves from legal pitfalls.

The Legal Foundations of Real Estate Law

The legal foundations of real estate law are rooted in common law principles, statutory regulations, and case law. These elements work together to create a comprehensive framework that governs property rights and transactions.

Common law, developed over centuries, provides the basis for many real estate principles. For example, the doctrine of "caveat emptor" (let the buyer beware) places the burden on buyers to perform due diligence before purchasing a property. While modern statutes have softened this principle, it remains a cornerstone of real estate law.

Statutory regulations build on common law by addressing specific issues such as zoning, environmental protection, and housing discrimination. Federal laws like the Fair Housing Act prohibit discrimination based on race, religion, or gender in housing transactions, ensuring equal access to housing opportunities. State and local laws further refine these rules, reflecting the unique needs of different communities.

Case law, derived from judicial decisions, plays a critical role in interpreting and applying real estate laws. For instance, court rulings often clarify ambiguous contract terms or establish precedents for resolving disputes. By studying case law, legal professionals can better understand how laws are applied in practice.

Together, these legal foundations provide the framework for a fair and functional real estate market. Understanding them is not only beneficial but necessary for anyone involved in property transactions.

Conclusion: Building a Foundation for Success

Real estate law is more than a set of rules, it's the foundation of every property transaction and decision. By understanding its importance, scope, key concepts, and legal foundations, you can approach property dealings with confidence and clarity.

This chapter has laid the groundwork for your journey into real estate law. The next chapter will explore property ownership, diving into the rights, responsibilities, and limitations that come with owning real estate. Whether you're a first-time buyer, a seasoned investor, or a curious reader, this book will equip you with the knowledge to succeed. Let's turn the page and continue building your expertise.

Chapter 2: Understanding Property Ownership

Introduction to Property Ownership

Property ownership is one of the cornerstones of real estate law, and understanding its nuances is essential for anyone involved in property dealings. Whether you're purchasing a home, leasing an apartment, or investing in commercial real estate, the type of ownership you hold significantly impacts your rights, responsibilities, and the decisions you make.

Ownership in real estate is not always straightforward. It can take various forms, from freehold estates that offer complete control over the property to leasehold rights that provide more limited access. Additionally, ownership comes with responsibilities, such as maintaining the property and complying with legal obligations like zoning laws and easements.

This chapter will delve into the types of property ownership, explaining the differences between freehold and leasehold rights. It will also explore the responsibilities of property owners, the legal definitions of ownership, and the limitations that zoning laws and easements can impose. By understanding these concepts, you'll be better equipped to navigate the complexities of property ownership and make informed decisions.

Types of Property Ownership

Property ownership is typically categorized into freehold estates and leasehold estates, each with distinct rights and limitations.

Freehold Ownership

A freehold estate is the most complete form of property ownership. It grants the owner full control over the property, including the rights to use, sell, lease, or pass it on to heirs. Freehold ownership is often associated with residential properties, where homeowners have the freedom to make decisions about their property without interference from others.

However, even freehold ownership has limitations. For example, zoning laws may restrict how the property can be used, and easements may grant others certain rights over the land. Additionally, freehold owners are responsible for property taxes, maintenance, and compliance with local regulations.

Freehold ownership can be further divided into two main types: fee simple and life estates. Fee simple ownership provides the most extensive rights, allowing the owner to use and transfer the property as they see fit. Life estates, on the other hand, grant ownership for the duration of an individual's life, after which the property typically passes to a designated beneficiary.

Leasehold Ownership

In contrast to freehold estates, a leasehold estate grants the right to use and occupy a property for a specified period, as outlined in a lease agreement. Leasehold ownership is common in commercial real estate and rental properties, where tenants pay rent in exchange for the right to use the property.

Leasehold rights are more limited than freehold rights. Tenants cannot sell or transfer the property, and their use of the property is often subject to restrictions set by the landlord. For example, a commercial tenant may be required to use the property only for business purposes and may need the landlord's permission to make significant modifications.

Despite these limitations, leasehold ownership offers flexibility. It allows individuals and businesses to occupy a property without the financial commitment of purchasing it outright. For landlords, leasehold arrangements provide a steady income stream and the ability to retain ownership of the property.

Understanding the differences between freehold and leasehold ownership is crucial for anyone involved in real estate. By knowing the rights and limitations associated with each type, you can make informed decisions about buying, leasing, or managing property.

Ownership Responsibilities

Owning property comes with significant responsibilities, regardless of whether you hold freehold or leasehold rights. These responsibilities are not only legal but also ethical, as they affect neighbors, communities, and the environment.

Maintenance and Upkeep

Property owners are responsible for maintaining their properties in a safe and habitable condition. This includes regular maintenance tasks such as repairing structural damage, addressing plumbing and electrical issues, and ensuring compliance with building codes. Failure to maintain a property can lead to legal consequences, including fines or lawsuits from tenants or neighbors.

For landlords, maintenance responsibilities often extend to ensuring that rental properties meet health and safety standards. This may include installing smoke detectors, addressing pest infestations, and ensuring proper ventilation. In many jurisdictions, landlords are legally required to respond to maintenance requests from tenants within a reasonable timeframe.

Financial Obligations

Property ownership also comes with financial responsibilities. Freehold owners must pay property taxes, which fund local services such as schools, roads, and public safety. Leasehold tenants, while not responsible for property taxes, may be required to pay rent, utilities, and other costs as outlined in their lease agreements.

Failure to meet financial obligations can result in serious consequences, such as foreclosure for freehold owners or eviction for leasehold tenants. Understanding these responsibilities is essential for managing property effectively and avoiding legal disputes.

Community and Environmental Impact

Property owners must also consider the impact of their actions on the surrounding community and environment. For example, building a commercial development in a residential neighborhood without proper permits can disrupt the community and lead to legal challenges. Similarly, failing to address environmental concerns, such as pollution or deforestation, can result in fines or lawsuits.

By fulfilling their responsibilities, property owners contribute to the well-being of their communities and the sustainability of the environment. This not only enhances their reputation but also protects the value of their investments.

Limitations on Ownership: Zoning Laws and Easements

While property ownership provides significant rights, it is not without limitations. Zoning laws and easements are two key factors that can restrict how property is used or developed.

Zoning Laws

Zoning laws are regulations that dictate how land in specific areas can be used. These laws are designed to ensure orderly development, promote public safety, and protect property values. For example, zoning laws may restrict certain areas to residential use while designating others for commercial or industrial purposes.

Zoning laws can significantly impact property ownership. For instance, a homeowner planning to convert their garage into a rental unit may need to obtain a zoning variance if local regulations prohibit such use. Similarly, a developer planning to build a shopping center must ensure that the land is zoned for commercial use.

Failure to comply with zoning laws can result in fines, legal action, or the forced removal of unauthorized structures. Understanding these regulations is essential for property owners and developers to avoid costly mistakes.

Easements

An easement is a legal right that allows someone to use a portion of another person's property for a specific purpose. Easements are common in real estate and can take various forms, such as utility easements, which grant utility companies the right to access private property for maintenance, or access easements, which allow neighbors to use a shared driveway.

While easements are often necessary, they can also create challenges for property owners. For example, a utility easement may prevent an owner from building on a specific part of their land, potentially limiting the property's value or usability. Additionally, disputes over easements can lead to legal conflicts, especially if the terms of the easement are unclear or contested.

Understanding easements and their implications is critical for property owners. By knowing the rights and limitations associated with easements, owners can navigate these challenges effectively and protect their investments.

Conclusion: Navigating Property Ownership

Owning property is a complex undertaking that involves a variety of rights, responsibilities, and potential restrictions. It is essential to understand key distinctions, such as the differences between freehold and leasehold ownership, as well as the legal responsibilities tied to property ownership. This includes navigating zoning regulations, understanding easements, and adhering to any covenants or restrictions that may apply. A solid grasp of these elements ensures that property owners can fulfill their obligations while protecting their investments.

For anyone involved in real estate, whether as a homeowner, landlord, tenant, or investor, having a clear understanding of property ownership is critical.

By mastering these concepts, you can make sound decisions, safeguard your assets, and reduce the risk of encountering legal challenges. This knowledge forms the backbone of success in real estate, equipping you to handle issues confidently and capitalize on opportunities in the property market.

In the following chapter, we'll shift our focus to navigating real estate transactions. By exploring the key elements of these processes, you'll gain valuable tools and practical insights to confidently manage the complexities of real estate deals.

Chapter 3: Navigating Real Estate Transactions

Introduction to Real Estate Transactions

Real estate transactions are among the most significant financial decisions individuals and businesses make. Whether you're buying your first home, selling a property, or transferring ownership, these processes involve a series of steps governed by legal and financial frameworks. Navigating these steps successfully requires a clear understanding of the procedures, documents, and obligations involved.

At the heart of any real estate transaction lies the goal of ensuring a smooth and fair exchange of property ownership. However, these transactions often feel overwhelming due to their complexity and the number of parties involved, including buyers, sellers, agents, attorneys, and lenders. Without proper preparation and knowledge, even minor mistakes can result in costly delays or legal disputes.

This chapter breaks down the step-by-step process of buying, selling, and transferring property. From title searches to closing, you'll gain a clear understanding of the essential legal elements that ensure successful transactions. By demystifying these processes, this chapter will equip you with the tools to navigate real estate transactions confidently and avoid common pitfalls.

Step One: Preparing for a Real Estate Transaction

The first step in any real estate transaction is preparation. This phase involves clarifying goals, understanding the market, and assembling the necessary resources to proceed.

Understanding Your Goals

Before initiating a transaction, it's important to define your objectives clearly. Are you buying a property as a primary residence, an investment, or a commercial space? If selling, are you aiming to maximize profit, downsize, or relocate? Clarifying your goals helps streamline the decision-making process and ensures you approach the transaction strategically.

Researching the Market

Market research is a critical aspect of preparation. For buyers, this involves identifying neighborhoods, comparing property prices, and evaluating market trends. Sellers, on the other hand, need to understand current market conditions to price their property competitively.

Real estate agents and online platforms can provide valuable insights during this phase. Additionally, working with a real estate attorney early in the process can help you understand local laws and regulations that may impact the transaction.

Securing Financing

For buyers, securing financing is a crucial part of preparation. This often involves obtaining a pre-approval letter from a lender, which outlines the loan amount you qualify for based on your income, credit score, and financial history. Pre-approval not only gives you a clearer picture of your budget but also demonstrates your seriousness as a buyer to sellers.

Sellers should also assess their financial position, especially if they plan to use the proceeds from the sale for another purchase. Understanding mortgage payoff amounts, taxes, and other costs associated with selling can prevent surprises later in the process.

Step Two: Conducting a Title Search

A title search is a critical step in any real estate transaction. This process ensures that the property in question has a clear title, free from liens, disputes, or other encumbrances that could affect ownership.

What is a Title Search?

A title search involves examining public records to verify the legal ownership of a property and identify any claims or restrictions on it. This process is typically conducted by a title company or real estate attorney. The goal is to ensure that the seller has the legal right to transfer ownership and that the buyer will receive a clean title.

Common Title Issues

Title searches can reveal a variety of issues, such as unpaid property taxes, undisclosed heirs, or easements that grant others rights to use the property. For example, a title search might uncover an unpaid lien from a previous owner, which could complicate the sale if not resolved.

Addressing title issues promptly is essential to avoid delays or legal disputes. In most cases, the seller is responsible for resolving these issues before closing. Title insurance, which protects buyers and lenders from financial loss due to title defects, is often purchased during this phase.

Step Three: Drafting and Negotiating the Contract

The purchase agreement, also known as the real estate contract, is the backbone of any transaction. This legally binding document outlines the terms and conditions of the sale, protecting the interests of both buyer and seller.

Key Components of a Real Estate Contract

A well-drafted contract includes several key elements:

- Purchase Price: The agreed-upon price for the property.
- Contingencies: Conditions that must be met for the sale to proceed, such as home inspections or financing approval.
- Closing Date: The date on which the transaction will be finalized.
- Earnest Money Deposit: A deposit made by the buyer to demonstrate their commitment to the transaction.

These elements ensure that both parties understand their obligations and minimize the risk of disputes.

Negotiating the Terms

Negotiation is an integral part of drafting the contract. Buyers may negotiate for repairs, price reductions, or extended timelines, while sellers might seek to limit contingencies or secure a higher deposit.

Working with experienced professionals, such as real estate agents and attorneys, can help you navigate negotiations effectively. Their expertise ensures that the contract reflects your interests while remaining legally enforceable.

Step Four: Closing the Transaction

The final step in a real estate transaction is closing, where ownership of the property is officially transferred from the seller to the buyer. Closing involves several critical tasks, from reviewing documents to disbursing funds.

The Closing Process

Closing typically takes place at a title company or attorney's office. During this process, the following steps occur:

1. Document Review: Both parties review and sign the necessary documents, including the deed, loan agreement, and closing disclosure.
2. Funds Disbursement: The buyer provides the funds for the purchase, while the seller receives the proceeds from the sale.
3. Transfer of Ownership: The deed is recorded with the local government, officially transferring ownership to the buyer.

Common Closing Challenges

Despite careful preparation, challenges can arise during closing. For example, a last-minute financing issue might delay the transaction, or an unexpected discrepancy in the closing statement could require additional negotiation.

To minimize these risks, it's important to stay organized and communicate regularly with all parties involved. Working with experienced professionals can also help ensure a smooth closing process.

Step Five: Post-Transaction Considerations

A real estate transaction doesn't end at closing. Both buyers and sellers have ongoing responsibilities that require attention.

For Buyers

After closing, buyers must ensure that they comply with their mortgage terms, maintain the property, and address any legal or financial obligations. For example, homeowners may need to pay property taxes, obtain insurance, or update zoning permits if they plan to renovate.

For Sellers

Sellers should retain copies of all transaction documents for tax purposes and address any outstanding liabilities, such as utility bills or HOA fees. Additionally, sellers may need to plan for capital gains taxes if the sale resulted in significant profit.

Understanding these post-transaction considerations ensures that both parties fulfill their obligations and avoid future disputes.

Conclusion: Mastering Real Estate Transactions

Real estate transactions may initially seem daunting, but with the right knowledge and preparation, they become not only manageable but also highly rewarding. Each stage of the process, preparing for a transaction, conducting a thorough title search, negotiating favourable terms, and closing the deal, is critical to ensuring a smooth and successful outcome. These steps form the foundation of any property transaction, and understanding them in detail allows you to approach the process with clarity and confidence.

Navigating real estate transactions requires attention to detail and a proactive mindset. By mastering the essential aspects of each phase, you can reduce risks, avoid costly mistakes, and secure the best possible results. Whether you're buying your first home, selling an investment property, or facilitating a complex deal, knowing what to expect at each stage can make all the difference.

This chapter has provided you with a comprehensive overview of the transaction process, equipping you with the knowledge and tools to handle real estate dealings effectively. However, the transaction process doesn't exist in isolation, it is deeply intertwined with the legal framework that underpins real estate. At the heart of every transaction are contracts and agreements, which serve as the binding elements that formalise the terms and protect the interests of all parties involved.

In the next chapter, we will delve into the intricate world of real estate contracts and agreements. From understanding the key clauses and terms to recognising potential red flags, you will gain insights into the legal foundation of real estate transactions. This deeper exploration will not only enhance your understanding of the process but also empower you to navigate the complexities of this dynamic field with even greater assurance. Whether you're entering into a simple purchase agreement or negotiating a sophisticated lease, a clear understanding of contracts and agreements is essential for success. Join us in the next chapter as we uncover the critical role these legal documents play in the world of real estate.

Chapter 4: Real Estate Contracts and Agreements

Introduction to Real Estate Contracts

Real estate contracts form the foundation of property transactions, acting as legally binding agreements that define the rights and responsibilities of all parties involved. Whether you're buying a home, leasing a property, or engaging in a commercial deal, understanding the components of these contracts is essential to protect your interests and ensure a successful outcome.

A well-drafted real estate contract does more than facilitate a transaction, it safeguards you from potential disputes and outlines a clear roadmap for the process. However, the legal language and complexity of these agreements can feel overwhelming, especially for those new to real estate.

This chapter explores the essential elements of real estate contracts, breaking down critical terms, contingency clauses, and negotiation strategies. By understanding these components, you'll gain the confidence to navigate agreements effectively and protect your interests at every stage.

Key Components of Real Estate Contracts

A real estate contract is composed of several key elements that establish the framework for the transaction. These components ensure that the agreement is clear, enforceable, and legally binding.

Offer and Acceptance

Every real estate contract begins with an offer, made by one party to another. The offer outlines the terms under which the property will be bought, sold, leased, or transferred. Once the other party agrees to these terms without modification, the offer is considered accepted, creating the foundation of a binding agreement.

For example, a buyer might offer to purchase a home for $300,000 with the condition that the seller repairs the roof before closing. If the seller agrees to these terms, the contract is formed. Any changes to the offer, such as a counteroffer from the seller, restart the negotiation process.

Consideration

Consideration refers to the value exchanged between the parties in a contract. In real estate transactions, this typically involves the buyer providing monetary payment in exchange for the property. However, consideration can also take other forms, such as services or goods.

For a contract to be legally enforceable, consideration must be present. Without it, the agreement is considered a gift rather than a binding contract.

Legal Purpose and Competence

A real estate contract must serve a legal purpose and involve parties who are legally competent to enter into an agreement. For instance, contracts involving illegal activities or made with minors are not enforceable.

Ensuring that all parties understand and agree to the terms of the contract is critical for its validity. This includes verifying that everyone involved has the mental and legal capacity to make informed decisions.

Understanding Contingency Clauses

Contingency clauses are conditions that must be met for a real estate contract to proceed. These clauses provide a level of protection for both buyers and sellers, ensuring that certain requirements are satisfied before the transaction is finalized.

Common Contingencies

- Inspection Contingency: Allows the buyer to conduct a property inspection and request repairs or renegotiate the price if issues are found.
- Financing Contingency: Protects the buyer if they are unable to secure a mortgage or other financing.
- Appraisal Contingency: Ensures the property is valued at or above the agreed-upon price,

allowing the buyer to renegotiate or withdraw if the appraisal falls short.
- Sale Contingency: Allows the buyer to complete the purchase only if they sell their current property within a specified timeframe.

These contingencies provide flexibility and safeguards, but they must be clearly defined to avoid confusion or disputes. For example, an inspection contingency should specify the timeline for inspections and the types of repairs that would allow the buyer to withdraw.

Balancing Contingencies

While contingencies offer protection, too many clauses can complicate the transaction and discourage the other party from proceeding. For instance, a seller might view a contract with multiple contingencies as risky and prefer an offer with fewer conditions.

Finding the right balance is key. Buyers should include contingencies that address significant risks, while sellers should seek to limit unnecessary conditions to streamline the process.

Negotiation Strategies

Negotiation is a critical aspect of real estate contracts, allowing parties to address their priorities, resolve conflicts, and reach a mutually beneficial agreement.

Preparing for Negotiation

Successful negotiation begins with preparation. Before entering discussions, identify your priorities, understand the other party's motivations, and gather relevant market data. For instance, a buyer might research comparable properties in the area to justify a lower offer, while a seller might highlight recent upgrades to support their asking price.

Working with a real estate agent or attorney can provide valuable insights during this phase. These professionals understand market trends and legal nuances, enabling you to approach negotiations with confidence.

Effective Communication

Clear and respectful communication is essential during negotiations. Focus on finding solutions rather than creating conflict, and be willing to compromise when necessary. For example, a seller might agree to lower the price in exchange for a faster closing, while a buyer might waive certain contingencies to make their offer more competitive.

Active listening is also important. By understanding the other party's perspective, you can identify opportunities for collaboration and build trust throughout the process.

Leveraging Contract Terms

Certain terms in the contract can be used as leverage during negotiations. For example, a buyer might request a price reduction if the inspection reveals significant issues, or a seller might offer a warranty to reassure the buyer and close the deal.

Understanding the implications of each term and how it affects the overall agreement is crucial for successful negotiation.

Ensuring Legal Enforceability

For a real estate contract to be legally enforceable, it must meet certain criteria. Failing to address these requirements can render the agreement invalid, leading to disputes or financial losses.

Clarity and Specificity

A legally enforceable contract must be clear and specific, leaving no room for ambiguity. Each term should be defined in detail, from the purchase price and payment schedule to the timeline for closing. For instance, instead of stating that the seller will make repairs, the contract should specify which repairs will be made, by whom, and within what timeframe.

Written Agreements

In most jurisdictions, real estate contracts must be in writing to be legally enforceable. Verbal agreements, while binding in some cases, are often difficult to prove and prone to disputes. Ensuring that all terms are documented in writing provides clarity and protection for both parties.

Signatures and Witnesses

A valid contract requires the signatures of all parties involved. In some cases, witnesses or notarization may also be required to enhance the contract's enforceability. For example, a deed transfer might require notarization to be recorded with the local government.

Compliance with Local Laws

Real estate contracts must comply with local laws and regulations. For instance, some jurisdictions require specific disclosures, such as lead paint hazards in older homes. Failing to include these disclosures can result in legal penalties or invalidate the contract.

Working with an experienced real estate attorney ensures that your contract meets all legal requirements and protects your interests.

Conclusion: Mastering Real Estate Agreements

Real estate contracts are far more than just legal documents, they are the cornerstone of every successful transaction. These agreements formalise the rights and obligations of all parties, setting the stage for a smooth and secure exchange of property. By understanding their essential components, such as key clauses, conditions, and contingencies, you can not only protect your interests but also approach negotiations with clarity and confidence. A strategic understanding of real estate contracts empowers you to identify potential issues, leverage opportunities, and ensure that each agreement aligns with your goals.

Each contract, whether for a sale, lease, or partnership, plays a pivotal role in the broader context of real estate law. Recognising how terms are structured and knowing when to negotiate or seek amendments can significantly influence the success of a transaction. The ability to navigate contracts thoughtfully helps minimise risks, streamline processes, and build a strong foundation for long-term success in the real estate market.

This chapter has provided an overview of real estate contracts, equipping you with practical tools to safeguard your interests and avoid common pitfalls. However, a deeper understanding of real estate law involves more than just mastering contracts. To truly thrive in this field, it's essential to grasp how external factors, such as zoning and land use regulations, influence what can and cannot be done with a property.

In Chapter 5: Zoning and Land Use Regulations, we'll delve into the critical role these laws play in shaping property development and usage. Zoning ordinances and land use rules govern everything from the types of structures that can be built on a property to how those structures can be used. Whether you're planning a residential development, opening a business, or simply making modifications to an existing property, these regulations determine the possibilities and limitations of your plans.

Understanding zoning and land use laws is not just about compliance, it's about strategic planning. These regulations can affect property values, investment potential, and even the feasibility of a project. By exploring this important topic, you'll gain valuable insights into how to assess properties, navigate local requirements, and align your real estate ventures with legal and planning frameworks.

Join me in the next chapter as we continue building your expertise, exploring how zoning and land use regulations form a critical link between real estate law and the practical realities of property ownership and development.

Chapter 5: Zoning and Land Use Regulations

Introduction to Zoning and Land Use

Zoning and land use regulations play a pivotal role in shaping how properties can be developed, used, and maintained. These laws, which are designed to balance individual property rights with the broader needs of the community, impact nearly every aspect of real estate. Whether you're a homeowner, developer, or investor, understanding zoning laws and land use restrictions is essential to avoid legal complications and maximize the potential of your property.

At their core, zoning laws establish specific guidelines for land use, dictating what types of structures can be built in certain areas and how those structures can be used. For example, zoning may designate some areas for residential use, others for commercial or industrial purposes, and still others for mixed-use development. These classifications aim to promote harmony, prevent conflicts, and ensure sustainable growth.

This chapter explores the legal framework governing property development and use, delving into zoning classifications, land use restrictions, and strategies for resolving disputes. By understanding these concepts, you'll gain the tools to navigate the complexities of zoning laws and make informed decisions about your property.

The Legal Framework of Zoning Laws

Zoning laws are established at the local level, typically by municipal or county governments, to regulate land use within their jurisdictions. These laws are rooted in police power, which allows governments to create regulations that protect public health, safety, and welfare.

The Purpose of Zoning

Zoning serves several key purposes:
- Promoting Orderly Development: Zoning ensures that land is used in a way that

promotes sustainable growth and prevents incompatible uses from disrupting neighborhoods. For instance, residential areas are typically separated from industrial zones to reduce noise and pollution.
- Protecting Property Values: By regulating land use, zoning helps maintain the character of neighborhoods and prevent activities that could devalue surrounding properties.
- Ensuring Public Safety: Zoning laws often include building codes and setback requirements to ensure structures are safe and accessible.
- Preserving Natural Resources: Environmental zoning protects sensitive areas such as wetlands, forests, and floodplains from overdevelopment.

Legal Authority

The legal authority for zoning laws originates from the Standard State Zoning Enabling Act (SSZEA), which grants local governments the power to regulate land use. This authority is further reinforced by court rulings, such as the landmark case Euclid v. Ambler Realty Co. (1926), which upheld the constitutionality of zoning laws.

By understanding the legal foundation of zoning, property owners and developers can better navigate the complexities of local regulations and avoid potential conflicts.

Zoning Classifications

Zoning classifications define how land can be used within a given area, creating distinct zones for residential, commercial, industrial, and other purposes.

Residential Zoning

Residential zones are designated for housing and related uses. They often include specific regulations governing the types of structures allowed, such as single-family homes, duplexes, or apartment buildings.

In addition to regulating building types, residential zoning may impose restrictions on lot sizes, building heights, and setback distances from property lines. For example, a local zoning code might require a minimum lot size of 10,000 square feet for single-family homes, ensuring that neighborhoods maintain a consistent density.

Commercial Zoning

Commercial zones are designated for business activities, including retail stores, restaurants, and offices. These zones often have specific requirements for parking, signage, and accessibility to ensure that commercial areas are functional and attractive.

For instance, a shopping center might be required to provide a certain number of parking spaces based on the square footage of its buildings. Additionally, commercial zoning may allow for mixed-use development, combining residential and commercial uses in a single area.

Industrial Zoning

Industrial zones are reserved for manufacturing, warehousing, and other heavy-use activities. These zones often have strict regulations to minimize environmental impact, such as limits on noise, emissions, and waste disposal.

For example, an industrial zone might require buffer zones between factories and residential areas to reduce noise and air pollution.

Special Zoning Categories

Some areas are designated as special zones to accommodate unique needs, such as historic preservation, environmental protection, or agricultural use. These zones often have additional regulations to protect their specific characteristics.

Understanding zoning classifications is essential for anyone involved in real estate, as they determine what can and cannot be done with a property.

Land Use Restrictions

In addition to zoning classifications, properties are often subject to land use restrictions that impose additional limitations on how they can be developed or used.

Easements

An easement is a legal right that allows someone to use a portion of another person's property for a specific purpose. Easements are common in real estate and can include utility easements, which grant utility companies the right to access private property for maintenance, or access easements, which allow neighbors to use a shared driveway.

While easements are often necessary, they can create challenges for property owners. For example, an easement might prevent a landowner from building on a specific part of their property, potentially limiting its value or usability.

Covenants

Covenants are agreements between property owners that impose certain restrictions on land use. For instance, a homeowners' association (HOA) might enforce covenants requiring residents to maintain their lawns or prohibit specific exterior paint colors.

Although covenants help maintain the character of neighborhoods, they can also limit individual property rights. Understanding these restrictions is essential for property owners to avoid conflicts and ensure compliance.

Environmental Regulations

Environmental regulations are another critical aspect of land use restrictions. These laws protect natural resources by limiting development in sensitive areas such as wetlands, forests, and floodplains. For example, a developer planning to build near a wetland might be required to obtain permits and implement mitigation measures to minimize environmental impact.

By understanding and addressing land use restrictions, property owners can navigate these challenges effectively and protect their investments.

Resolving Zoning Disputes

Zoning disputes can arise when property owners, developers, or neighbors disagree about land use regulations. Resolving these disputes requires a thorough understanding of the legal framework and a strategic approach.

Common Causes of Zoning Disputes

Zoning disputes often involve:

- Nonconforming Uses: When a property is used in a way that does not comply with current zoning laws, such as a business operating in a residential zone.
- Variance Requests: When a property owner seeks an exception to zoning regulations,

such as a smaller setback distance or increased building height.
- Boundary Disputes: When neighbors disagree about property lines or encroachments.

Strategies for Resolution

- Administrative Appeals: Many zoning disputes can be resolved by appealing to a local zoning board or planning commission. These bodies have the authority to grant variances, approve special permits, or interpret zoning codes.
- Negotiation and Mediation: In some cases, disputes can be resolved through direct negotiation or mediation, allowing the parties to reach a mutually agreeable solution without litigation.
- Litigation: If other methods fail, zoning disputes may be resolved in court. This option is typically more time-consuming and expensive but may be necessary for complex or high-stakes cases.

Understanding the options available for resolving zoning disputes empowers property owners to protect their interests and find effective solutions.

Conclusion: Mastering Zoning and Land Use

Zoning and land use regulations are not just legal requirements, they are essential tools for creating harmony between individual property rights and the broader needs of a community. These laws govern how land can be developed and used, shaping everything from residential neighbourhoods to commercial hubs. By understanding zoning classifications, restrictions, and processes for resolving disputes, you can confidently navigate these regulations and make decisions that align with your goals. Whether you're planning a development project, considering a property purchase, or simply looking to modify your existing property, a solid grasp of these laws is crucial.

Every zoning decision carries implications for property value, usability, and future potential. What type of zoning applies to your property? Are there restrictions that could impact your plans? What opportunities might zoning variances open up for your investments? These are just some of the questions that zoning and land use regulations can help answer. By understanding how these rules work, you empower yourself to act strategically and ensure compliance while maximising the value of your real estate ventures.

This chapter has laid a foundation by exploring the legal framework that governs property development and use. But what happens when you need to finance a property or development project? How do you navigate the complexities of mortgages, liens, and the risks of foreclosure? Financing is the lifeblood of real estate, and understanding the legal and financial aspects of borrowing is critical for success.

In the next chapter, "Mortgages, Financing, and Liens," we'll take a deep dive into the world of real estate financing. You'll learn how mortgages work, explore different financing options, and gain insights into the rights and responsibilities of both borrowers and lenders.

Chapter 6: Mortgages, Financing, and Liens

Introduction to Real Estate Financing

Real estate financing is one of the most critical components of property transactions, enabling individuals and businesses to purchase properties they might not otherwise afford. However, the legal and financial intricacies of mortgages, liens, and foreclosure processes can feel overwhelming without a solid understanding of the rules that govern them.

At its core, financing involves borrowing money to fund the purchase of real estate, with the property itself serving as collateral. While this system opens the door to homeownership and investment opportunities, it also comes with risks and obligations. Borrowers must navigate a maze of legal agreements, repayment terms, and potential consequences if they fail to meet their obligations.

This chapter explores the legal aspects of real estate financing, breaking down the components of mortgages, the implications of liens, and the foreclosure process. You'll also gain practical advice on understanding borrowers' rights and navigating financial agreements effectively.

Understanding Mortgages

A mortgage is a legal agreement between a borrower and a lender, allowing the borrower to purchase property by securing a loan. In exchange, the lender holds a claim to the property as collateral until the loan is fully repaid. Mortgages are the most common form of real estate financing, and understanding their structure is essential for buyers and investors.

Components of a Mortgage

A typical mortgage agreement includes several key components:

- Principal: The original loan amount borrowed by the buyer.
- Interest: The cost of borrowing money, expressed as a percentage of the principal.

- Term: The length of time over which the loan will be repaid, typically 15 or 30 years.
- Amortization Schedule: A breakdown of payments, showing how much goes toward the principal and interest over time.

Understanding these components allows borrowers to evaluate mortgage offers and choose the one that best fits their financial situation. For example, a lower interest rate may result in significant savings over the life of the loan, while a shorter term may lead to higher monthly payments but quicker equity buildup.

Types of Mortgages

Mortgages come in various forms, each tailored to different borrower needs:

- Fixed-Rate Mortgages: Offer a consistent interest rate and monthly payment over the life of the loan.
- Adjustable-Rate Mortgages (ARMs): Feature an initial fixed rate that adjusts periodically based on market conditions.
- Government-Backed Mortgages: Loans insured by government agencies such as the Federal Housing Administration (FHA) or Department of Veterans Affairs (VA),

designed to help first-time buyers or those with limited resources.

Choosing the right mortgage type depends on factors such as income stability, long-term plans, and risk tolerance. Borrowers should carefully consider their options and consult with financial advisors or real estate professionals to make informed decisions.

The Role of Liens in Real Estate

A lien is a legal claim or right against a property, typically used to secure payment for a debt. In real estate, liens play a significant role in protecting lenders and other creditors, ensuring that they can recover their funds if the borrower defaults.

Types of Liens

Liens can be classified into two main categories: voluntary liens and involuntary liens.

- Voluntary Liens: These are created with the consent of the property owner, such as a mortgage lien. In this case, the lender holds

a claim to the property as collateral for the loan.
- Involuntary Liens: These are imposed without the owner's consent, often due to unpaid debts or legal judgments. Examples include tax liens, mechanic's liens, and judgment liens.

Implications of Liens

Liens can significantly impact property transactions. For instance, a property with an unresolved lien cannot be sold or refinanced until the lien is satisfied. This makes it essential for buyers and sellers to conduct thorough title searches to identify any liens on the property before completing a transaction.

In some cases, liens can lead to foreclosure if the debt remains unpaid. For example, a homeowner with a tax lien who fails to pay their taxes may lose their property through a tax sale. Understanding the implications of liens and how to address them is crucial for protecting your investments.

Navigating Foreclosure

Foreclosure is the legal process through which a lender takes ownership of a property when the borrower fails to meet their mortgage obligations. While foreclosure is often seen as a last resort, it is a significant risk for borrowers who fall behind on payments.

The Foreclosure Process

The foreclosure process typically involves the following steps:

1. Notice of Default: The lender notifies the borrower that they have missed payments and must bring their account current within a specified timeframe.
2. Pre-Foreclosure: If the borrower does not resolve the default, the lender begins the foreclosure process. During this stage, the borrower may have the opportunity to sell the property or negotiate with the lender.
3. Foreclosure Sale: The property is sold at auction to recover the outstanding debt. In some cases, the lender may take ownership of the property if no suitable buyer is found.

4. Eviction: If the property is occupied, the new owner may initiate eviction proceedings to remove the occupants.

Avoiding Foreclosure

Borrowers facing financial difficulties should take proactive steps to avoid foreclosure. Options include:

- Loan Modification: Negotiating new terms with the lender, such as extending the loan term or reducing the interest rate.
- Forbearance: Temporarily pausing or reducing payments to give the borrower time to recover financially.
- Short Sale: Selling the property for less than the outstanding loan balance, with the lender's approval.

Understanding these options and seeking professional advice can help borrowers navigate financial challenges and avoid the long-term consequences of foreclosure.

Borrowers' Rights and Obligations

Borrowers have specific rights and obligations under real estate financing agreements. Knowing these rights ensures that borrowers are treated fairly, while fulfilling obligations helps maintain a positive relationship with lenders.

Borrowers' Rights

Borrowers are entitled to certain protections, including:

- Fair Lending Practices: Lenders must comply with laws such as the Equal Credit Opportunity Act (ECOA) and Fair Housing Act, which prohibit discrimination in lending.
- Clear Disclosure: Borrowers have the right to receive clear and accurate information about loan terms, fees, and repayment schedules.
- Right to Cancel: In some cases, borrowers can cancel certain types of loans within a specified period, such as refinancing agreements.

Borrowers' Obligations

In addition to rights, borrowers have obligations that must be fulfilled to maintain their financing agreements:

- Timely Payments: Borrowers must make monthly payments on time, including principal, interest, taxes, and insurance (PITI).
- Property Maintenance: Borrowers are responsible for maintaining the property to protect its value, as it serves as collateral for the loan.
- Compliance with Loan Terms: Borrowers must adhere to all terms outlined in the loan agreement, such as maintaining adequate insurance coverage.

Understanding and fulfilling these obligations helps borrowers avoid penalties, maintain good credit, and protect their investments.

Practical Advice for Navigating Financing

Navigating real estate financing requires careful planning and informed decision-making. The following tips can help borrowers make the most of their financing opportunities:

Assess Your Financial Situation

Before applying for a mortgage, evaluate your financial situation to determine how much you can afford. Consider factors such as your income, expenses, credit score, and savings for a down payment.

Shop Around for Lenders

Don't settle for the first lender you encounter. Compare offers from multiple lenders to find the best terms, including interest rates, loan fees, and repayment options.

Understand the Fine Print

Read your loan agreement carefully and ask questions about any terms you don't understand.

This ensures that you're fully aware of your obligations and potential risks.

Plan for the Long Term

Consider how your financial situation might change over time and choose a mortgage that aligns with your goals. For example, if you plan to move within a few years, an adjustable-rate mortgage might be more cost-effective than a fixed-rate loan.

By following these strategies, borrowers can navigate the complexities of real estate financing with confidence and achieve their property goals.

Conclusion: Mastering Real Estate Financing

Mortgages, liens, and foreclosure processes are foundational components of real estate financing, influencing every aspect of property transactions, from purchasing and ownership to resolving financial disputes. These mechanisms provide the framework through which properties are bought, sold, and maintained, often serving as the financial backbone of real estate ventures. Understanding these concepts is essential for anyone involved in property transactions, whether you're a first-time homebuyer, an experienced investor, or a developer managing multiple projects.

Mortgages, in particular, represent a pivotal step in securing financing. What types of mortgage options are available, and how do their terms impact your financial strategy? Understanding the nuances of fixed-rate versus adjustable-rate mortgages, prepayment penalties, and refinancing opportunities can make a significant difference in how you approach borrowing. Similarly, liens, whether voluntary or involuntary, affect your property's title and can have serious implications for your financial and legal standing. Do you know how to identify potential liens on a property? More importantly, do you know how to resolve them?

Foreclosure is another critical aspect of real estate financing, and while it is a situation most strive to avoid, understanding the process is vital. What are your rights as a borrower in the foreclosure process? What legal protections might be available, and how can you negotiate with lenders to mitigate financial losses? By mastering these areas, you equip yourself to make informed decisions, safeguard your investments, and navigate the complexities of real estate financing with confidence.

This chapter has provided an exploration of real estate financing, giving you the tools and insights needed to approach financial agreements strategically and protect your property investments. But financing is only one piece of the puzzle. Once a property is purchased and ownership established, another critical aspect of real estate law comes into play: rental property management.

In the next chapter, "Legal Issues in Rental Properties," we will dive into the intricate dynamics of landlord-tenant relationships, focusing on lease agreements, tenant rights, and the legal obligations of property owners.

As we move forward, think about how rental properties fit into your real estate strategy. What challenges might you face in navigating landlord-tenant laws? How can you structure lease agreements to protect both parties while maintaining a positive relationship? Let's continue this journey together, building your expertise in real estate law and preparing you for the dynamic and rewarding world of rental property management.

Chapter 7: Legal Issues in Rental Properties

Introduction to Legal Issues in Rental Properties

The rental property market is a dynamic and vital part of the real estate industry, serving millions of landlords and tenants across the United States. However, the relationship between landlords and tenants is governed by a complex web of laws designed to protect the rights and responsibilities of both parties. Understanding these legal frameworks is crucial for ensuring fair treatment, minimizing disputes, and fostering a productive rental relationship.

Whether you're a landlord managing multiple properties or a tenant renting your first apartment, navigating the nuances of landlord-tenant law, lease agreements, and dispute resolution can be challenging. Misunderstandings or violations of these laws often lead to legal disputes, financial losses, or damaged relationships.

This chapter explores the rights and responsibilities of landlords and tenants, delves into the components of legally binding lease agreements, and examines common disputes within the rental framework. By understanding these principles, you can navigate the rental property landscape with confidence and clarity.

The Foundation of Landlord-Tenant Relationships

The relationship between landlords and tenants is regulated by state and local laws, which provide a legal framework for property rental. These laws aim to balance the rights and responsibilities of both parties, ensuring that tenants enjoy safe and habitable housing while landlords maintain control over their properties.

Key Rights of Tenants

Tenants are entitled to several fundamental rights under landlord-tenant law:

- Right to Habitability: Landlords must provide rental properties that meet basic health and safety standards. This includes functioning plumbing, heating, and electrical systems, as

well as protection from hazards like mold or pests.
- Right to Privacy: Tenants have the right to enjoy their rental property without unnecessary interference from the landlord. Most states require landlords to provide notice before entering the property, except in emergencies.
- Protection from Discrimination: The Fair Housing Act prohibits landlords from discriminating against tenants based on race, religion, gender, disability, or other protected characteristics.

Key Rights of Landlords

Landlords also have specific rights to protect their investments and maintain order on their properties:

- Right to Payment: Landlords are entitled to receive rent payments on time, as specified in the lease agreement.
- Right to Evict: In cases of nonpayment, lease violations, or illegal activities, landlords have the right to initiate eviction proceedings, provided they follow proper legal procedures.
- Right to Property Maintenance: Landlords can set rules regarding property use to

ensure it is well-maintained and complies with local regulations.

By understanding these rights, both landlords and tenants can foster a respectful and legally compliant rental relationship.

Lease Agreements: The Cornerstone of Rental Relationships

A lease agreement is a legally binding contract that defines the terms and conditions of the rental relationship. This document protects both parties by outlining their rights, responsibilities, and expectations.

Key Components of a Lease Agreement

A comprehensive lease agreement includes the following elements:

- Identification of Parties: Names and contact information for the landlord and tenant(s).

- Property Description: The address and details of the rental property, including any included amenities or furnishings.
- Rent Terms: The amount of rent, due date, acceptable payment methods, and penalties for late payments.
- Security Deposit: The amount required, conditions for its return, and allowable deductions.
- Lease Term: The duration of the lease, whether it's month-to-month, annual, or another specified period.
- Use of Property: Rules regarding how the property can be used, such as prohibiting subleasing or specific activities.
- Maintenance and Repairs: Responsibilities for maintaining the property and addressing repairs, including who is responsible for what.

By clearly defining these terms, lease agreements help prevent misunderstandings and disputes. For instance, specifying who is responsible for landscaping or appliance repairs can eliminate confusion and ensure accountability.

Legal Requirements for Leases

Lease agreements must comply with local and state laws to be enforceable. For example:

- Some states cap the amount landlords can charge for security deposits.
- Certain jurisdictions require landlords to include disclosures about lead-based paint or other hazards.
- Lease agreements must avoid illegal terms, such as waiving the tenant's right to a habitable property.

Consulting with a real estate attorney can ensure that your lease agreement meets legal standards and protects your interests.

Common Disputes in Rental Properties

Despite clear agreements and good intentions, disputes between landlords and tenants are common. Understanding the root causes of these conflicts and how to address them is essential for maintaining a positive rental relationship.

Nonpayment of Rent

One of the most frequent disputes arises when tenants fail to pay rent on time. While this can result from financial hardship or simple oversight, landlords must follow legal procedures to address the issue.

For example, most states require landlords to provide written notice before initiating eviction proceedings. This notice typically gives the tenant a specific timeframe to pay the overdue rent or vacate the property.

Maintenance and Repairs

Disagreements over maintenance responsibilities are another common source of conflict. Tenants may argue that landlords are neglecting necessary repairs, while landlords may claim that tenants caused the damage.

Clear communication and documentation are critical in these situations. Tenants should submit maintenance requests in writing, and landlords should respond promptly and document all actions taken.

Security Deposit Disputes

Disputes often arise over the return of security deposits. Tenants may feel that deductions are unfair or excessive, while landlords may argue that the deductions are justified.

To avoid disputes, landlords should provide an itemized list of deductions and supporting documentation, such as receipts or photos of damage. Tenants should conduct a walkthrough with the landlord at the beginning and end of the lease to document the property's condition.

Resolving Rental Disputes

When disputes arise, resolving them quickly and fairly is in the best interests of both parties. Several strategies can help address conflicts within the legal framework.

Communication and Negotiation

Open and respectful communication is often the simplest way to resolve disputes. By discussing the issue calmly and seeking a compromise, landlords and tenants can often find mutually agreeable solutions.

For example, if a tenant is struggling to pay rent, the landlord might agree to a payment plan or temporary rent reduction in exchange for the tenant's commitment to catch up on payments.

Mediation

If direct negotiation fails, mediation can provide a neutral forum for resolving disputes. A mediator helps both parties communicate effectively and explore potential solutions, without imposing a decision.

Mediation is often faster and less expensive than litigation, making it an attractive option for resolving rental disputes.

Legal Action

In cases where disputes cannot be resolved through communication or mediation, legal action may be necessary. Landlords can file for eviction, while tenants can sue for damages if they believe their rights have been violated.

Before pursuing legal action, both parties should consult with an attorney to understand their options and potential outcomes.

Rights and Responsibilities of Each Party

Both landlords and tenants have specific rights and responsibilities that shape their rental relationship. Understanding and fulfilling these obligations is essential for maintaining compliance with the law and fostering mutual respect.

Landlord Responsibilities

Landlords are responsible for:

- Providing a safe and habitable property that meets local housing codes.
- Responding to maintenance requests promptly and addressing health or safety hazards.
- Respecting tenants' privacy and providing proper notice before entering the property.

Tenant Responsibilities

Tenants are responsible for:

- Paying rent on time and in full, as outlined in the lease agreement.
- Keeping the property clean and in good condition, beyond normal wear and tear.
- Complying with lease terms, such as rules regarding pets or subleasing.

By understanding and fulfilling all of these responsibilities, landlords and tenants can reduce the likelihood of disputes and create a positive rental experience.

Conclusion: Navigating Legal Issues in Rental Properties

The legal framework surrounding rental properties plays a critical role in balancing the rights and responsibilities of landlords and tenants. These laws are designed to foster fair treatment, transparency, and accountability, creating a stable foundation for rental relationships. For landlords, understanding the intricacies of lease agreements, tenant rights, and property maintenance obligations is essential for managing properties effectively and avoiding potential conflicts. For tenants, knowledge of their rights ensures they can advocate for fair treatment and hold landlords accountable when necessary.

Crafting clear and legally sound lease agreements is one of the most important aspects of rental property management. A well-drafted lease outlines the expectations, responsibilities, and rights of both parties, minimising misunderstandings and providing a framework for resolving potential issues. What clauses should be included to protect your interests? How can you structure a lease to comply with local laws while maintaining flexibility for unforeseen circumstances? These are essential questions for anyone involved in rental property arrangements.

Even with the best preparations, disputes can arise. Whether it's disagreements over rent increases, security deposits, or maintenance obligations, effectively addressing these issues requires a solid understanding of landlord-tenant laws and a proactive approach to conflict resolution. Mediation, arbitration, or legal action may sometimes be necessary to resolve disputes, but a clear and cooperative communication strategy can often prevent conflicts from escalating. How can landlords and tenants work together to foster positive relationships? What strategies can help resolve disagreements before they reach the courts?

This chapter has provided an exploration of the legal issues surrounding rental properties, equipping you with the tools to navigate these relationships confidently. However, legal challenges in real estate extend beyond the immediate concerns of leases and tenant management. Disputes, whether between landlords and tenants, property developers and municipalities, or buyers and sellers, are an inevitable part of the industry. Understanding how to resolve these conflicts effectively is critical for long-term success.

In the next chapter, "Dispute Resolution and Future Trends," we'll delve into the strategies and processes used to address conflicts in real estate, from negotiation and mediation to litigation and arbitration. As you continue this journey, consider the broader implications of dispute resolution in the real estate sector. How can you prepare to navigate disputes while staying ahead of industry changes? What steps can you take to integrate these trends into your real estate strategy? Let's move forward with these questions in mind, building a deeper understanding of the dynamic and ever-evolving world of real estate law.

Chapter 8: Dispute Resolution and Future Trends

Introduction to Dispute Resolution and Future Trends

Disputes are an inevitable part of real estate, arising from misunderstandings, conflicting interests, or legal violations. Whether the issue involves a boundary disagreement, a breach of contract, or zoning violations, resolving these conflicts requires a solid understanding of dispute resolution methods. In parallel, the real estate industry is evolving rapidly, with technological advancements and sustainability-focused regulations reshaping the landscape.

This chapter explores the key methods for resolving real estate disputes, including mediation, arbitration, and litigation, providing guidance on when and how to use each approach. It also delves into the future of real estate law, examining how technology and sustainability initiatives are driving change and creating new opportunities.

By understanding both dispute resolution strategies and emerging trends, you'll gain a comprehensive perspective on navigating real estate challenges while preparing for the industry's future.

Methods of Resolving Real Estate Disputes

Disputes in real estate can range from minor disagreements to complex legal battles. Choosing the right resolution method depends on the nature of the conflict, the stakes involved, and the willingness of the parties to cooperate.

Mediation: Collaborative Problem-Solving

Mediation is a voluntary and collaborative process in which a neutral third party, known as a mediator, assists disputing parties in reaching a mutually acceptable resolution. Unlike the rigid and often adversarial nature of litigation, mediation provides a more flexible and informal setting where parties can openly discuss their concerns and interests. The mediator facilitates communication, helps identify common ground, and guides the discussion toward a solution that benefits all parties involved.

One of the key advantages of mediation is its focus on preserving relationships, which is particularly important in real estate disputes involving ongoing partnerships, landlord-tenant relationships, or community development projects. By fostering a cooperative environment, mediation encourages creative problem-solving and allows parties to retain control over the outcome, rather than leaving decisions in the hands of a judge or arbitrator.

Mediation is also highly cost-effective compared to litigation, reducing both financial expenses and the time required to resolve disputes. Its informal nature eliminates much of the procedural complexity associated with court cases, enabling parties to focus on resolving the core issues at hand. Furthermore, because mediation sessions are private and confidential, they provide a safe space for candid discussions, which can lead to more durable and satisfactory agreements.

This process is well-suited to a wide range of real estate disputes, including disagreements over property boundaries, lease terms, construction delays, and even homeowner association conflicts.

By avoiding the adversarial approach of court proceedings, mediation not only saves time and money but also reduces the emotional strain that often accompanies legal disputes. Ultimately, mediation empowers parties to craft tailored solutions that meet their specific needs and goals, creating a more positive and productive path to conflict resolution.

The Mediation Process

During mediation, the mediator facilitates discussions between the parties, encouraging open communication and creative problem-solving. The goal is to identify common ground and negotiate a solution that satisfies both sides.

For example, a landlord and tenant disputing over unpaid rent might agree to a payment plan during mediation, avoiding the need for eviction proceedings.

Benefits of Mediation

Mediation offers several advantages:

- Confidentiality: Discussions remain private, protecting sensitive information.

- Control: The parties retain control over the outcome, rather than leaving it to a judge or arbitrator.
- Preservation of Relationships: Mediation fosters collaboration, making it ideal for ongoing relationships, such as between neighbors or business partners.

Mediation is particularly effective for disputes involving personal relationships or low-stakes conflicts, where cooperation is possible.

Arbitration: A Middle Ground

Arbitration is a more formal process than mediation, involving a neutral arbitrator who hears evidence and makes a binding or non-binding decision. It combines elements of mediation and litigation, offering a faster and less expensive alternative to court proceedings.

The Arbitration Process

Arbitration begins with both parties agreeing to submit their dispute to an arbitrator, often as part of a pre-existing contract clause. The arbitrator reviews evidence, hears arguments, and issues a decision, which may be binding or non-binding depending on the agreement.

For instance, a dispute between a developer and contractor over construction delays might be resolved through arbitration, with the arbitrator determining responsibility and compensation.

Benefits and Drawbacks

Arbitration offers several benefits:

- Efficiency: Cases are resolved more quickly than in court.
- Expertise: Arbitrators often have specialized knowledge of real estate or construction.
- Flexibility: The process can be tailored to the needs of the parties.

However, arbitration has drawbacks, such as limited opportunities for appeal and potential bias if the arbitrator is chosen by one party. It is best suited for commercial disputes or cases where speed and expertise are priorities.

Litigation: The Courtroom Approach

Litigation is the most formal method of dispute resolution, involving a court trial to determine the outcome. While litigation is often seen as a last resort due to its cost and time requirements, it is sometimes necessary for resolving complex or high-stakes disputes.

The Litigation Process

Litigation begins with one party filing a lawsuit against the other. The process includes:

1. Filing a Complaint: The plaintiff outlines the dispute and their desired resolution.
2. Discovery: Both parties gather evidence, including documents, witness statements, and expert testimony.
3. Trial: A judge or jury hears the case and issues a binding decision.
4. Appeal: Either party may appeal the decision if they believe errors were made.

Litigation is often used in cases involving significant financial stakes, such as disputes over property ownership or breach of contract.

Pros and Cons of Litigation

Litigation offers the advantage of a definitive, enforceable outcome. However, it comes with significant drawbacks, including high costs, lengthy timelines, and public exposure. It is best reserved for disputes that cannot be resolved through other means.

Emerging Trends in Real Estate Law

As the real estate industry evolves, legal frameworks must adapt to new challenges and opportunities. Two key trends shaping the future of real estate law are technological innovations and sustainability-focused regulations.

Technological Innovations

Technology is transforming real estate transactions, making them faster, more efficient, and transparent. Tools like blockchain enable secure, automated processes through smart contracts, reducing intermediaries and fraud. Virtual tours and augmented reality allow buyers to explore properties remotely, while AI streamlines tasks such as document processing and valuations. E-signature platforms and cloud-based systems simplify paperwork, cutting delays and improving accessibility. These advancements are revolutionising the industry, offering a seamless and more user-friendly experience for all parties involved.

Blockchain Technology

Blockchain is revolutionizing property transactions by creating secure, transparent, and immutable records. Smart contracts, self-executing agreements coded on the blockchain, reduce the need for intermediaries, speeding up transactions and reducing costs.

For example, blockchain can simplify the title transfer process by providing a tamper-proof record of ownership, minimizing the risk of disputes.

Artificial Intelligence (AI)

AI is enhancing decision-making in real estate by analyzing large datasets to identify trends, predict property values, and assess market conditions. AI-powered tools can also streamline contract drafting and review, reducing errors and ensuring compliance with legal standards.

Virtual Reality (VR)

VR technology is transforming property marketing by allowing buyers to explore properties remotely. This innovation is particularly valuable for international transactions or during travel restrictions.

By embracing these technologies, the real estate industry can improve efficiency, reduce costs, and enhance the customer experience.

Sustainability-Focused Regulations

Sustainability is becoming a central focus in real estate law, driven by environmental concerns and changing consumer preferences.

Green Building Standards

Many jurisdictions are adopting green building codes that require new constructions to meet energy efficiency and sustainability criteria. For instance, the Leadership in Energy and Environmental Design

(LEED) certification promotes sustainable practices in design, construction, and operation.

Renewable Energy Incentives

Governments are offering incentives for incorporating renewable energy systems, such as solar panels, into properties. These incentives not only reduce environmental impact but also increase property value and attract eco-conscious buyers.

Climate Resilience Regulations

As climate change poses increasing risks, real estate laws are addressing issues such as floodplain management, wildfire mitigation, and disaster preparedness. These regulations aim to protect both property owners and the environment.

Understanding and complying with sustainability-focused regulations is essential for staying competitive in the evolving real estate market.

Integrating Dispute Resolution and Future Trends

As the real estate industry embraces innovation and sustainability, dispute resolution methods must also adapt. Technology offers new tools for resolving disputes, such as online mediation platforms and AI-driven arbitration. Additionally, sustainability regulations may give rise to new conflicts, such as disputes over compliance costs or environmental impact assessments.

By staying informed about these trends and embracing innovative approaches, property owners, developers, and professionals can navigate challenges effectively and seize opportunities in the evolving real estate landscape.

Conclusion: Preparing for the Future of Real Estate

Real estate disputes are a common occurrence in a field as dynamic and multifaceted as real estate. Whether they involve disagreements over property boundaries, lease terms, construction delays, or contractual obligations, conflicts can disrupt transactions and relationships if not handled effectively. Understanding dispute resolution methods, such as mediation, arbitration, and litigation, is essential for navigating these challenges. Mediation, with its collaborative approach, allows parties to reach mutually agreeable solutions while preserving relationships. Arbitration offers a structured yet flexible alternative to litigation, providing a binding resolution without the delays and costs of court proceedings. Litigation, while often a last resort, remains a critical option for resolving disputes that cannot be settled through other means.

At the same time, the real estate industry is being reshaped by technological innovations and sustainability-focused regulations. Blockchain technology, smart contracts, virtual tours, and AI-driven platforms are revolutionising how transactions are conducted, offering unprecedented speed, security, and transparency. These tools not only streamline processes but also provide new opportunities to enhance accuracy and efficiency in managing real estate dealings. Meanwhile, the rise of sustainability initiatives has introduced new standards for property development, requiring professionals to consider energy efficiency, green building practices, and environmental impact in their projects. These trends create both challenges and opportunities, demanding adaptability and forward-thinking strategies.

This chapter has offered an exploration of both dispute resolution methods and the emerging trends that are shaping the future of real estate law. Equipped with these insights, you are better prepared to address conflicts efficiently, embrace innovation, and navigate the evolving legal and regulatory landscape of the industry. However, even with the best tools and knowledge, success in real estate requires vigilance and a commitment to continuous learning.

As you move forward, it is equally important to be aware of common mistakes that can undermine your efforts. In Chapter 9: Common Mistakes to Avoid, we will delve into the pitfalls that many real estate professionals, investors, and property owners encounter, from overlooking critical contract details to mismanaging due diligence or failing to adapt to market changes. What are the most frequent missteps in real estate transactions, and how can you avoid them? How can you identify and mitigate risks before they escalate into larger issues?

By examining these mistakes, you'll gain practical advice on how to refine your strategies and make informed decisions that protect your interests. Let's continue this journey together, equipping you with the knowledge and tools to succeed in this ever-changing industry while avoiding the challenges that can derail even the most well-intentioned plans.

Chapter 9: Common Mistakes to Avoid

Introduction to Common Mistakes in Real Estate

Real estate transactions, whether renting, buying, or selling, are often complex and fraught with potential pitfalls. Even small oversights can lead to significant financial losses, legal disputes, or missed opportunities. For landlords, tenants, buyers, and property owners, understanding these common mistakes and how to avoid them is crucial for success in the world of real estate.

This chapter explores the most frequent errors made in real estate, from neglecting due diligence to mismanaging lease agreements or ignoring legal obligations. By identifying these mistakes and providing actionable advice to address them, this chapter aims to equip you with the tools to navigate real estate transactions confidently and avoid unnecessary risks.

Mistakes Landlords Often Make

Landlords play a critical role in the rental process, but their actions (or inactions) can have long-lasting consequences. Below are common mistakes landlords make and how to prevent them.

Inadequate Screening of Tenants

One of the most frequent mistakes landlords make is failing to properly screen potential tenants. Accepting a tenant without verifying their credit history, income, or references can lead to financial loss or legal disputes.

How to Avoid This Mistake

- Conduct thorough background checks, including credit reports and criminal history.
- Verify employment and income to ensure the tenant can meet rent obligations.
- Speak to previous landlords for insight into the tenant's behavior.

By prioritizing tenant screening, landlords can reduce the risk of late payments, property damage, and eviction proceedings.

Poorly Written Lease Agreements

A poorly written or incomplete lease agreement often leads to confusion and disputes between landlords and tenants. For example, failing to specify maintenance responsibilities or late payment penalties can create unnecessary tension.

How to Avoid This Mistake

- Use a legally compliant lease template or consult an attorney to draft the agreement.
- Clearly outline all terms, including rent amount, due dates, security deposit details, and maintenance obligations.
- Ensure both parties sign the lease and retain copies for future reference.

A strong lease agreement serves as a foundation for a healthy landlord-tenant relationship.

Mistakes Tenants Often Make

Tenants, too, face challenges in navigating rental agreements and responsibilities. Understanding common errors can help tenants avoid legal and financial troubles.

Ignoring the Lease Terms

Tenants often fail to read their lease agreements thoroughly, leading to misunderstandings about their rights and obligations. For instance, a tenant might unknowingly violate a no-pets policy or miss deadlines for giving notice to vacate.

How to Avoid This Mistake

- Take the time to read the lease agreement in full, asking questions about unclear terms.
- Pay attention to clauses about security deposits, late fees, and property use restrictions.
- Keep a copy of the lease for reference throughout the tenancy.

Being informed about lease terms helps tenants avoid costly mistakes and maintain a positive relationship with their landlord.

Skipping the Move-In Inspection

Another common mistake tenants make is neglecting the move-in inspection, which documents the property's condition at the start of the lease. Failing to complete this step can result in disputes over security deposit deductions at the end of the tenancy.

How to Avoid This Mistake

- Conduct a detailed walkthrough of the property with the landlord before moving in.
- Take photos or videos of any pre-existing damage and share them with the landlord for documentation.
- Request a written move-in inspection report, signed by both parties.

A thorough move-in inspection protects tenants from being held responsible for damage they did not cause.

Mistakes Buyers Often Make

Buying property is one of the most significant financial decisions most people make, yet many buyers fall into avoidable traps that can derail the process.

Skipping the Home Inspection

One of the costliest mistakes buyers make is forgoing a home inspection, often to save time or money. Without an inspection, buyers may overlook serious issues such as structural damage, mold, or faulty plumbing.

How to Avoid This Mistake

- Hire a licensed home inspector to evaluate the property thoroughly.
- Attend the inspection to ask questions and gain insight into the property's condition.
- Use the inspection report to negotiate repairs or adjust the purchase price.

Investing in a home inspection is a small price to pay for peace of mind and long-term savings.

Overextending Financially

Another common mistake is buying more property than one can afford, often driven by emotion rather than financial planning. Overextending financially can lead to mortgage default or foreclosure.

How to Avoid This Mistake

- Get pre-approved for a mortgage to understand your budget.
- Factor in additional costs such as property taxes, insurance, and maintenance.
- Stick to properties within your financial means, even if larger or more expensive options are tempting.

Staying within your budget ensures that homeownership remains a positive experience rather than a financial burden.

Mistakes Sellers Often Make

Selling property requires careful planning and strategy, but many sellers make errors that reduce their profitability or delay the sale process.

Overpricing the Property

Setting an unrealistically high price is one of the most common mistakes sellers make. Overpriced properties tend to sit on the market longer, discouraging potential buyers and eventually requiring price reductions.

How to Avoid This Mistake

- Conduct a comparative market analysis (CMA) to determine a competitive price.
- Work with a real estate agent to assess market trends and buyer demand.
- Be willing to adjust the price based on feedback and market conditions.

Pricing the property appropriately increases the likelihood of a quick and profitable sale.

Neglecting to Stage the Property

Sellers who fail to stage their property effectively may struggle to attract buyers. Cluttered or poorly maintained spaces can leave a negative impression, even if the property has potential.

How to Avoid This Mistake

- Clean and declutter the property, focusing on creating a welcoming and neutral environment.
- Make minor repairs and updates, such as painting walls or replacing worn carpets.
- Consider hiring a professional stager to highlight the property's best features.

Staging helps buyers visualize themselves in the space, increasing the chances of a successful sale.

General Legal Mistakes to Avoid

In addition to role-specific errors, there are general legal mistakes that landlords, tenants, buyers, and sellers should avoid to ensure compliance with real estate laws.

Failing to Conduct a Title Search

Whether buying, selling, or leasing property, neglecting a title search can lead to legal complications. Title searches reveal liens, ownership disputes, and other issues that could jeopardize the transaction.

How to Avoid This Mistake

- Work with a title company or attorney to conduct a thorough title search.
- Address any issues uncovered during the search, such as unpaid liens or unclear ownership.
- Obtain title insurance to protect against unforeseen claims.

A clear title is essential for a smooth and legally sound transaction.

Ignoring Local Zoning Laws

Overlooking zoning laws and land use restrictions can result in fines, project delays, or the need to modify plans. For example, building a commercial property in a residential zone without proper permits can lead to legal action.

How to Avoid This Mistake

- Research local zoning regulations before purchasing or developing property.
- Consult with zoning experts or attorneys to ensure compliance.
- Apply for variances or permits if necessary to proceed with your plans.

Understanding zoning laws minimizes the risk of legal challenges and project disruptions.

Conclusion: Learning from Common Mistakes

Real estate transactions, whether renting, buying, selling, or managing properties, are filled with opportunities, but also potential pitfalls. As this chapter has demonstrated, even minor missteps, such as neglecting a move-in inspection, underestimating the importance of tenant screening, or failing to conduct a title search, can lead to significant financial losses, legal disputes, and strained relationships. These common mistakes, while costly, are entirely avoidable with proper preparation, awareness, and attention to detail.

For landlords, creating clear lease agreements and thoroughly screening tenants lays the groundwork for successful rental relationships. For tenants, carefully reading lease terms and documenting the property's condition protects their rights and ensures transparency. Buyers benefit from conducting home inspections and adhering to realistic budgets, while sellers achieve better results by pricing properties competitively and staging them effectively. Across all roles, understanding local zoning laws and conducting title searches are fundamental steps to prevent legal complications and ensure compliance.

Avoiding these mistakes not only safeguards your investments but also builds trust and confidence among all parties involved. Real estate success often hinges on the ability to anticipate challenges, mitigate risks, and act with foresight and clarity. The actionable strategies outlined in this chapter are designed to help you make informed decisions and navigate real estate transactions with greater confidence.

As we conclude this chapter, it's important to take a step back and reflect on the broader lessons learned. What common mistakes might you already be making, and how can you address them proactively? What steps can you take to ensure that each future transaction is smoother and more successful than the last?

In the next and final chapter, "Final Thoughts," we will tie together the insights and strategies explored throughout this book. Real estate is a complex and ever-evolving field, but with the right mindset and knowledge, you can turn challenges into opportunities. Let's reflect on the journey so far and explore how to apply these lessons to build lasting success in real estate. As you move forward, remember: preparation, adaptability, and a commitment to continuous learning are the keys to thriving in this dynamic industry. Let's continue this journey together and solidify the foundation for your real estate success.

Chapter 10: Final Thoughts and Summary of Main Points

Reflecting on the Journey Through Real Estate Law

As we come to the conclusion of this book, it's important to reflect on the journey we've taken together through the dynamic and often complex world of real estate law. From the foundational principles that underpin property ownership to the advanced strategies for navigating disputes and embracing future trends, each chapter has built upon the last, offering a comprehensive introduction to this vital field.

Real estate law is not just about contracts and transactions, it's about empowering individuals to make informed decisions, protect their rights, and achieve their goals, whether they're buying their first home, managing a rental property, or embarking on a major development project. This final chapter serves as a summary of the key insights from the book, tying together the lessons learned and providing a roadmap for applying this knowledge in real-world scenarios.

Understanding the Importance of Real Estate Law

In Chapter 1, we explored the foundational role of real estate law in everyday life. This chapter introduced the scope and significance of real estate law, emphasizing its impact on property transactions, financial decisions, and the broader community.

The legal framework that governs real estate is designed to balance individual property rights with societal needs. By understanding these principles, you're better equipped to navigate the complexities of property dealings, from securing ownership to resolving disputes.

The introduction also highlighted the importance of being proactive and informed. Real estate law is not something to approach passively, it requires diligence, curiosity, and a willingness to seek expert advice when needed. This mindset sets the stage for success in every aspect of real estate.

Mastering Property Ownership

Chapter 2 delved into the different types of property ownership, including freehold and leasehold rights, and the responsibilities that come with owning property. Understanding the nuances of property ownership is essential for making informed decisions, whether you're purchasing a home, leasing an apartment, or investing in commercial real estate.

This chapter also emphasized the importance of being aware of zoning laws, easements, and other restrictions that can impact property use. These legal considerations can significantly influence the value and usability of a property, making them critical factors in any real estate transaction.

The insights from this chapter underscore the importance of due diligence. By thoroughly researching a property and its legal status, you can avoid costly surprises and ensure that your investment aligns with your goals.

Navigating Real Estate Transactions

In Chapter 3, we broke down the step-by-step process of buying, selling, and transferring property. This chapter demystified complex concepts such as title searches, escrow, and closing, providing a clear roadmap for successful transactions.

One of the key takeaways from this chapter was the importance of clear communication and documentation. Real estate transactions involve multiple parties, each with their own interests and responsibilities. Ensuring that everyone is on the same page helps prevent misunderstandings and keeps the process moving smoothly.

The chapter also highlighted the value of working with professionals, such as real estate agents, attorneys, and title companies. These experts bring valuable knowledge and experience to the table, helping you navigate challenges and protect your interests.

Crafting Effective Contracts

Chapter 4 focused on real estate contracts and agreements, which form the backbone of any property transaction. This chapter explored the components of legally binding contracts, including key terms, contingency clauses, and negotiation strategies.

A recurring theme in this chapter was the importance of clarity and specificity. Ambiguities in a contract can lead to disputes or unintended consequences, making it essential to define terms clearly and address potential scenarios in advance.

The chapter also emphasized the need for thorough review and understanding of contracts. Whether you're a buyer, seller, landlord, or tenant, taking the time to review the terms of an agreement, and seeking legal advice if necessary, can save you from significant challenges down the road.

Navigating Zoning and Land Use Regulations

Chapter 5 delved into the zoning and land use regulations that shape how properties can be developed and used. This chapter highlighted the role of zoning laws in promoting orderly development, protecting property values, and ensuring public safety.

A key takeaway from this chapter was the importance of understanding zoning classifications and land use restrictions before purchasing or developing property. Failure to comply with these regulations can result in fines, delays, or even the loss of your investment.

The chapter also explored strategies for resolving zoning disputes, emphasizing the value of communication, negotiation, and, when necessary, legal action. These insights are particularly valuable for developers and investors navigating the complexities of land use planning.

Managing Mortgages, Financing, and Liens

In Chapter 6, we explored the legal aspects of mortgages, financing, and liens, providing a comprehensive overview of how these elements shape real estate transactions.

This chapter highlighted the importance of understanding the terms and conditions of financing agreements, from interest rates and loan terms to amortization schedules. By being informed, borrowers can make smarter decisions and avoid common pitfalls, such as overextending financially or failing to meet repayment obligations.

The discussion of liens and foreclosure processes underscored the need for vigilance and proactive management. Whether dealing with voluntary liens like mortgages or involuntary liens such as tax liens, understanding the implications and addressing issues promptly can protect your investment and financial stability.

Navigating Legal Issues in Rental Properties

Chapter 7 shifted the focus to rental properties, exploring the rights and responsibilities of landlords and tenants. This chapter provided practical insights into drafting lease agreements, managing disputes, and maintaining compliance with landlord-tenant laws.

A key takeaway was the importance of clear and legally compliant lease agreements. These documents set the foundation for a successful rental relationship, minimizing misunderstandings and ensuring that both parties understand their obligations.

The chapter also addressed common disputes, such as maintenance issues and security deposit disagreements, offering strategies for resolution through communication, negotiation, and, when necessary, legal action.

Resolving Disputes and Embracing Future Trends

Chapter 8 explored methods for resolving real estate disputes, including mediation, arbitration, and litigation, as well as emerging trends in real estate law. This chapter emphasized the value of choosing the right dispute resolution method based on the nature of the conflict and the parties' willingness to cooperate.

The discussion of future trends highlighted the transformative impact of technology and sustainability-focused regulations on the real estate industry. From blockchain technology and artificial intelligence to green building standards and renewable energy incentives, these innovations are reshaping how properties are bought, sold, and managed.

Understanding and adapting to these trends is essential for staying competitive in the evolving real estate landscape.

Learning from Common Mistakes

Chapter 9 rounded out the book by exploring the common mistakes made by landlords, tenants, buyers, and sellers in real estate transactions. This chapter offered practical advice for avoiding these pitfalls, from conducting due diligence to crafting clear contracts and maintaining open communication.

The overarching message of this chapter was the importance of preparation and education. By learning from the experiences of others and staying informed about legal requirements, you can navigate the complexities of real estate with confidence and success.

Final Takeaways

As we conclude, it's clear that real estate law is both a practical tool and a powerful safeguard. Whether you're an individual homeowner, a landlord managing multiple properties, or a developer embarking on a large-scale project, understanding the principles and practices outlined in this book will serve you well.

The real estate market is constantly evolving, shaped by legal frameworks, economic forces, and technological innovations. Staying informed and adaptable is key to navigating these changes and achieving your goals.

This book is not just a guide, it's a starting point. Use the knowledge you've gained here as a foundation for further exploration, and don't hesitate to seek professional advice when faced with complex or high-stakes decisions.

Thank you for taking this journey through real estate law. With the tools and insights you've gained, you're well-equipped to navigate the challenges and opportunities of the real estate world with confidence and clarity.

Acknowledgements

Writing this book has been a journey of exploration, learning, and collaboration, and it would not have been possible without the support and contributions of so many remarkable individuals.

First, I want to express my deep gratitude to the attorneys, legal professionals, and advisors I have had the privilege of working with over the years. Your expertise and dedication have not only guided my understanding of real estate law but also inspired me to share this knowledge with a wider audience. Thank you for your unwavering commitment to clarity, fairness, and the pursuit of justice in every legal process.

To the individuals who made themselves available for interviews, shared insights, and provided invaluable assistance during the research and writing of this book, you know who you are, thank you for your time, openness, and generosity. Your contributions have enriched this work in ways words cannot fully express.

I am equally grateful to my school teachers and university lecturers, whose lessons laid the foundation for my legal thinking. You instilled in me the importance of structure, critical analysis, and the value of approaching problems with a thoughtful and disciplined mindset.

Finally, to anyone who has ever been part of a legal process, whether as a professional, a participant, or a witness, thank you for contributing to the broader understanding of how law shapes our lives. Your experiences and perspectives serve as vital reminders of the human side of legal practice.

This book is as much a reflection of your efforts and wisdom as it is of my own. Thank you all.

Glossary of Keywords

Real estate is a constantly evolving industry that demands continuous learning and adaptability. Staying informed about the latest trends and understanding key terminology is essential for success. This glossary is designed to enhance your knowledge of real estate and real estate law, equipping you with some of the vocabulary needed to navigate this dynamic field with confidence and expertise.

A

- Adjustable-Rate Mortgages (ARMs): Mortgages with an interest rate that changes periodically.
- Affidavit: A written statement confirmed by oath or affirmation, used as evidence in court.
- Amortization Schedule: A table detailing payments of principal and interest over a loan term.
- Appraisal: Evaluation of a property's value, typically for financing or sale purposes.

- Arbitration: A dispute resolution process where a neutral party makes a binding or non-binding decision.

B

- Boundary Disputes: Disagreements over property lines between neighbors.
- Borrower Obligations: Duties that borrowers must fulfill under loan agreements, such as timely payments.
- Building Codes: Standards for construction, maintenance, and safety of structures.

C

- Capital Gains Tax: Tax on the profit from the sale of property or investments.
- Comparative Market Analysis (CMA): A report used to estimate property value based on recent sales.
- Contingency Clauses: Conditions that must be met for a contract to proceed, such as inspection requirements.
- Covenants: Agreements restricting how property can be used.
- Closing Costs: Fees associated with finalizing a property transaction.

- Contracts: Legally binding agreements that outline terms and responsibilities.

D

- Deeds: Legal documents that transfer property ownership from seller to buyer.
- Default: Failure to meet legal or financial obligations, such as loan payments.
- Disclosures: Mandatory information about a property, such as known defects or hazards.
- Dispute Resolution: Methods for resolving disagreements, including mediation, arbitration, and litigation.

E

- Easements: Legal rights for someone to use another's property for specific purposes.
- Escrow: A neutral third party holds funds or documents until conditions of a contract are met.
- Eviction: Legal process of removing a tenant from a rental property.

F

- Fair Housing Act: U.S. law prohibiting discrimination in housing based on protected characteristics.

- Financing: Securing funds, typically through loans, for purchasing property.
- Fixed-Rate Mortgages: Loans with consistent interest rates and payments throughout the term.
- Foreclosure: Legal process where a lender takes possession of a property due to default.

G

- Green Building Standards: Regulations promoting environmentally friendly construction practices.
- Gross Income: Total earnings before deductions, often used in evaluating mortgage eligibility.

H

- Habitable Conditions: Minimum standards of safety and livability for rental properties.
- Home Inspection: Assessment of a property's condition before purchase.
- Homeowner's Association (HOA): Organization managing shared spaces and rules in a community.

I

- Insurance Requirements: Policies, such as homeowner's insurance, required by lenders or lease agreements.
- Interest Rates: The cost of borrowing money, expressed as a percentage of the loan amount.

J

- Judgment Liens: Legal claims on property resulting from court judgments.

K

- Key Terms: Crucial concepts in real estate law, such as zoning, liens, and contingencies.

L

- Land Use Restrictions: Regulations governing how property can be developed or used.
- Lease Agreements: Contracts outlining terms and conditions between landlords and tenants.
- Liens: Legal claims against property as collateral for debt.
- Litigation: Court-based resolution of disputes.

M

- Mediation: A collaborative process to resolve disputes with a neutral third party.
- Mixed-Use Zoning: Designation allowing multiple uses, such as residential and commercial, on the same property.
- Mortgages: Loans secured by property used to finance real estate purchases.

N

- Negotiation Strategies: Techniques for reaching agreements in transactions or disputes.
- Nonconforming Use: Existing property use that doesn't comply with current zoning laws.

O

- Occupancy Permits: Certificates verifying a property meets safety and zoning requirements.

P

- Property Taxes: Annual taxes levied by local governments based on property value.
- Purchase Agreements: Contracts for buying property, detailing terms and contingencies.

Q

- Quitclaim Deed: A legal document transferring ownership without guaranteeing title quality.

R

- Renewable Energy Incentives: Financial benefits for using solar or other sustainable energy systems.
- Rental Disputes: Conflicts between landlords and tenants over lease terms or property conditions.
- Rights of Tenants: Legal protections ensuring fair treatment and habitable conditions.

S

- Security Deposits: Funds held by landlords to cover potential damage or unpaid rent.
- Setback Requirements: Rules specifying how far buildings must be from property lines.
- Sustainability Regulations: Laws promoting energy efficiency and environmental protection in real estate.

T

- Tax Liens: Claims by the government for unpaid property taxes.
- Title Insurance: Protection against financial loss due to title defects or disputes.
- Title Searches: Reviews of public records to confirm property ownership and identify encumbrances.

U

- Utilities Easements: Rights allowing utility companies to access private property for maintenance.

V

- Variance Requests: Appeals to modify zoning restrictions for specific projects.

W

- Walkthrough Inspections: Final checks of property condition before purchase or lease begins.

Z

- Zoning Laws: Local regulations defining property use, such as residential, commercial, or industrial.
- Zoning Disputes: Conflicts over property use or development restrictions.

Author Bio

With decades of hands-on experience in real estate, Willem brings a wealth of practical insights to his readers. Known for his helpful, informative, and concise style, Willem aims to guide both novice and experienced readers through the complexities of real estate with clarity and reliability. Outside of his professional life, he enjoys staying active, keeping up with fitness, and spending time with his wife, sharing a love for good food and sports. Readers can trust his expertise and find in him a reliable resource for real estate knowledge they can apply with confidence.

Social Profiles and Contact Info

I'd love to stay connected and continue the conversation. You can find me on LinkedIn and X (formerly Twitter) to keep up with my latest projects, insights, and resources. I'm also available for face-to-face consultations, public speaking, and group training sessions via Whatsapp, Zoom, Google Meet, or Microsoft Teams.

Feel free to reach out on any of these platforms to connect, share ideas, or discuss opportunities for learning and growth. Let's keep building together!

LinkedIn: https://www.linkedin.com/in/willemtait/
X (previously Twitter): https://x.com/willemtait
Calendly: https://calendly.com/willemtait
Email: willemtait@outlook.com

Public Speaking, Mentorship, Consulting, Coaching

As a dedicated professional with a passion for real estate, business, law, and economics, I thrive on sharing actionable insights and practical strategies that empower individuals and teams to achieve their goals. My expertise spans real estate investment, business consulting, personal growth, and the intricate connections between legal and economic frameworks, allowing me to offer a well-rounded perspective tailored to diverse challenges and ambitions.

Through public speaking engagements, customised mentorship programs, and dynamic one-on-one or group coaching sessions, I aim to inspire, educate, and guide. Whether addressing an audience of hundreds or working closely with a small team, my mission is to deliver value-driven insights that leave a lasting impact.

If you're seeking a keynote speaker to energise and inform your event, a consultant to elevate your business strategies, or a mentor to foster personal and professional growth, I'm here to collaborate. My approach integrates years of hands-on experience with a solid foundation in real estate, law and economics, ensuring the strategies I share are both practical and informed by robust principles.

Let's connect to explore how I can help you or your organisation unlock new opportunities and achieve meaningful success. Together, we can create strategies that inspire growth, drive innovation, and deliver measurable results.

LinkedIn: https://www.linkedin.com/in/willemtait/

Mail: willemtait@outlook.com

Upcoming Projects

Thank you for joining me on this journey into the fascinating world of real estate. This book is just the first step in what I hope will be a long and meaningful exploration of the strategies, insights, and opportunities that define the real estate landscape.

I'm excited to share that my next book is already well underway. It builds upon the foundation laid here, diving deeper into the complexities of real estate investment, development, and market dynamics. Backed by even more in-depth research and practical case studies, this upcoming work will provide actionable advice and fresh perspectives designed to empower your success in this ever-evolving field.

We Value Your Feedback!

Thank you for taking the time to read *Practical Principles of Commercial Real Estate Investment*. Your insights and experiences with this book mean the world to me, and I would love to hear your thoughts.

If you found the strategies and principles in this book helpful, please consider leaving a review on Amazon or your preferred platform. Your feedback not only helps me improve but also helps other readers discover valuable resources for their commercial real estate journey.

Sharing your thoughts can inspire others to take the next step in their investment journey. Whether it's a quick rating or a detailed review, your voice makes a difference!

Thank you again for your time and trust in this book. Wishing you success in all your real estate ventures!

Portfolio of Books by Willem Tait

For more, kindly see www.amazon.com/author/willemtait

BUSINESS BOOKS

1. **Real Estate Law Essentials:** Navigate Cross-Sections, Avoid Pitfalls, and Seize Opportunities.
2. **Proven Principles of Residential Real Estate Investment:** Strategies and Tasks for Building Generational Wealth.
3. **Practical Principles of Commercial Real Estate Investment:** Tasks and Strategies for Real Estate Success.
4. **Real Estate Economics:** Property Market Principles and Practices.
5. **Raising Money for Real Estate Investment:** Close Deals, Raise Money, Build Wealth.
6. **Capital Markets and Real Estate:** How Money and Capital Shapes the Property Market.
7. **Real Estate Development and Deal Making:** The Essential Guide for Property Developers, Entrepreneurs, and Dealmakers.
8. **Psychology of Residential and Commercial Real Estate:** Master the Psychology Behind Real Estate Success.
9. **Philosophy of Residential and Commercial Real Estate:** Exploring the Intersection of Philosophy, People, Property, Purpose and Spaces.
10. **Economics of Banking and Money:** Insight into Power, Trust, and Change.
11. **The Future of Real Estate:** PropTech, Sustainability and Design

SELF-HELP AND MOTIVATIONAL BOOKS

1. **Sort Your Crap Out:** Own Your Choices, Silence Your Critic. Get Stuff Done
2. **Dammit, Get It Together:** Stop Making Excuses and Start Living the Life You Deserve
3. **Stop Giving a Damn and Start Living:** Cut the Crap. Focus on What Matters. Live Fully
4. **Dammit, It's Your Life:** Own Your Mind, Time, and Choices
5. **Dammit, Stop Being Overwhelmed and Overworked:** Reclaim Your Time, Energy, and Sanity

ANNOTATED AND COMMENTARY

1. **The Way to Wealth** (Annotated): With Motivational Commentary by Willem Tait
2. **The Art Of War:** (Annotated): Proven Modern Strategies for Winning in Business, Leadership, and Life by Willem Tait

www.ingramcontent.com/pod-product-compliance
Lightning Source LLC
Chambersburg PA
CBHW071548220526
45469CB00003B/946